All rights reserved. This book may not be reproduced in whole or in part, stored in a retrieval system, or transmitted in any form or by any means electronic, mechanical, or other without written permission of the author, except by reviewer, who may quote brief passages with source information in a review.

Cover and interior design: Nathalie Turgeon
Photo: Nathalie Turgeon
ISBN Library and Archives Canada Paperback: 978-1-7380358-2-3
French version: Affirmations du matin - Gloire du matin
Translation: Nathalie Turgeon

*An affirmation can be like the beautiful
Morning Glory flower, which opens to its full potential
as it energizes with each sunrise.
Take the time to connect
to your Inner and True Self.*

It's not always easy to control our mental space.

But when we know how to tell the difference between what comes from our ego and what comes from our Soul, our inner Self or Higher Self, we can more quickly regain control of our thoughts and our well-being.

- Do you have a mental overflow?
- Do you mostly see the negative scenario before the positive possibility?
- Do you tend to imagine this negative scenario in its smallest details?
- Do you have a desire, if not a need, to believe in yourself a little more?
- Do your negative beliefs about yourself sometimes or often take up too much mental space?
- Did you know that your inner Self is pure positivity, and that your ego may be in the way, or a little too much in control, when it should be your ally in the passenger seat?

Without delving into the more metaphysical details and explanations of what the ego is, having a different perception of one's thoughts helps to open up to more. And this more opens up in different ways and at different times for each of us.

I created this program to help you better understand your mental space in a very simplified way. It is a little like the basis of a mindfulness journey. **Each day you are brought to be aware of what you are automatically feeding.** One day at a time you are invited to know yourself better through your mental space. Little by little, you are brought to understand and accept that "you can" choose your thoughts, the ones you feed because you will know which thoughts do not allow you to be in harmony with your inner Self, therefore, to create your life according to your deep desires. For 31 days, I invite you to become the observer of your mental space.

Personally, for my equilibrium and my mental health, I had to learn to control my mental space and I quickly understood that my ego is always in survival mode and puts me in a constant state of survival, so it was up to me to take control of my thoughts and those I fed, but also to learn to listen to the message that a negative thought brings. The more I understood my ego, the more I understood that every negative thought hides a fear which was keeping me in some ego-comfort. This book does not talk about these messages, but I strongly encourage you to take the time... to take the time to listen to them to delete them, because **we do not overcome our fears, we delete them**. They are not real; they are the fruit of the ego in action to remain in ego-comfort.

An ego-comfort can easily become a golden prison.

It is by understanding what comes from my ego and what comes from my Soul, my inner Self that I regained control of my mental space, but also that I regained confidence in myself to follow my dreams, knowing that I could and can achieve them.

What helped me the most was seeing the thoughts coming from the ego clearly.

I strongly encourage you to do these 31 days of mindfulness by following the 31 affirmations, one affirmation per day, to gently, without triggering the control of your ego, better connect with your magnificent and powerful inner Self, or even better reconnect to a new level of mindfulness. Well-being is a lifelong process.

We always start from *point A* which is today, your present moment. It is simple and only takes a few minutes a day. I take you from your *point A* to your *point B* one day at a time.

Enjoy your mindfulness journey!

Dr. Nathalie Turgeon Ph.D. *Metaphysical Practitioner*

Why 31 Days of mindful Affirmations?

Every day, everything we do, everything we think about and spend time with is what serves to create our tomorrow. **We create our tomorrow from the beliefs we have in the present moment.** An old belief that we believe today, without changing it, also becomes a belief of the present moment. When we think it would be good to do something, we generate desired and less desired consequences. When we think it would be good not to do something for xyz reasons, we generate consequences, good and not so good, corresponding to what we believe.

Our beliefs shape our life and our tomorrow.

Our beliefs also shape who we are and what we do.

Our beliefs are very often false and obsolete, but we continue to nurture them, we keep them active as if our life depended on them.

Guess what? It depends on them. This part is correct. Hence the reason to change the beliefs that do not correspond to what we want to live tomorrow.

What if I told you that every time you feel negative about yourself, your situation, or your life, there is some kind of positive counterpart. Would you like to see and experience this positive counterpart? What if I told you that the "you", the ego-you that you call "me" which can be very negative and sometimes lacks confidence and love, also has a positive counterpart. Would you like to meet this positive person filled with creative power?

Well, I invite you to meet your totally positive and confident inner Self, one day at a time. In fact, it will take you a lifetime to fully meet your inner Self and begin to believe and trust unconditionally that part of you, which is your Authentic Self, but all you need is to take the first step and begin to see who this inner Self is.

The ego-me, a vocabulary to understand the difference here, very often will use negative beliefs to prevent you from stepping out of the comfort box, or your safety zone, coming from your ego where the ego directs you. The ego takes over the mental space easily so that you stay in an ego-comfort zone, and yes, you allow your ego to rule you without always being aware of it. When the ego is in control, you may feel that what you desire is impossible and beyond your reach because of and from your beliefs.

Often these limiting beliefs are negative, or they are beliefs that we have adopted either from our education, from those around us or from an experience we have had. When we experience something, we establish beliefs about what we are experiencing as we experience it. These beliefs resurface in our mental space when we experience the same thing or something very similar again.

Our beliefs shape our life and our tomorrow.
Our beliefs also shape who we are and what we do.
Our beliefs are very often false and obsolete,
but we continue to feed them, we keep them active.

Our beliefs are stored in our personal database, our subconscious, and when we face something, in fact everything, our conscious mind takes its information from our database to know what to think and how to react, it is therefore up to us to change these beliefs, or to activate those that we prefer and would like to have in order to better create our future.

In a few words, our inner Self is pure positivity. Everything that is negative comes from our ego, and everything that is positive but conditionally positive also comes from our ego.

Our Soul, our inner Self or our Divine Self, as you prefer to call it, is pure positivity and infinitely powerful in its source.

I invite you to take the time... to take the time every day for the next 31 days to meet your inner Self, to change your thoughts as well, and to begin to change your story. You are doing this for no one else but yourself, for your well-being.

A felt affirmation gives a more positive result.

Have you ever noticed how certain affirmations seem to make you feel better and more powerful? It is because you felt them. They were not just random affirmations you repeated to please your ego. And often, they were also affirmations that reminded you of your Authentic Self, your inner Self. I must mention here, however, that too often, affirmations only please the ego. Over the next 31 days, you will be led to better see what comes from your ego to better write your own affirmations and also to adhere to those that will help you feel more in harmony with yourself.

One of the first steps to living in harmony with oneself is to learn what is false and what is true, therefore what comes from the ego and what comes from the inner Self or the Soul. To say that everything from the ego is wrong here is somewhat referring to the concept that the ego occupies the mental space for its own survival and purposes, and not for the well-being of your Higher Self. Mental space can only serve one at a time, either the ego for its own well-being which is temporary and conditional, or the well-being of your Higher Self and the well-being of all, the Greater good.

An affirmation is something that one affirms, declares, thinks, or says by perceiving what one thinks as being "the" truth. **It is something we believe or "think" we believe**. It can be something you want to believe eventually hence the reason for repetitive affirmations as a well-being practice. And it is quite possible to think that this is "the only" truth, and that everyone must or should think and say the same thing, and have the same perception, including oneself when one adheres to the affirmation from someone else.

An affirmation can be as much negative as positive since it is simply affirming something that we believe.

A negative affirmation is an affirmative and negative sentence, clearly asserting negativity. It is a negative and clear judgment that one has about others or oneself. It is a negative judgment that we choose to believe.

An affirmation can be positive and conditional on something. It still makes it an affirmation, even if it is ego-conditional. It is something that is affirmed and/or believed and that pleases the ego for the *xyz* reasons. We can even build a whole life from positive, but ego-conditional affirmations.

When we affirm something, we are making a declaration of a deeply held belief that we have, or we are declaring what we have been taught as a belief to be integrated regardless of the reason for which we ended up believing it. **An affirmation that we repeat and express in our present moment is a belief that we have "chosen" to believe in our present moment.** The beauty is that all beliefs can be changed, without exception. A belief is just a belief.

When we affirm something, we do so either fully aware or mechanically without awareness or knowledge of the scope of the vocabulary used.

When a person states or affirms something that they believe, they will tend to begin their sentence with the word "I" such as: "I believe that", "I think that", "I can", "I cannot", "I am", "I am not", "I prefer", "I like", "I do not like". The "I" can also be *you*, he, she, we, they.

The words that follow are simply a statement based on personal judgment. These judgments may be so deeply embedded that one does not even remember where they came from or why one decided to believe the belief one is asserting.

We may also have heard a sentence so often that we do not even realize the harmful effect it can have on our psychic atmosphere, that is to say the atmosphere that surrounds us and which is interconnected.

Why harmful? Because what follows the word "I" or "I cannot" comes to determine what the person is creating, that is to say his or her reality.

A person saying "I think life is good" or a person saying "I think life is crap" are creating the following in their reality and ego-vision. Not only can the ego not disagree with itself, but words come with specific emotions and energetic frequencies.

A person who affirms "I am able to…" and a person who affirms "I am not able to…" will not have the same result nor the same journey before reaching this result. They will not have the same challenges or obstacles to overcome. Their mental space will be occupied by thoughts justifying what is asserted. These thoughts will influence actions and inactions. An affirmation is made up of words, and these words come with personal perceptions or definitions, associations and emotions.

An affirmation can be both negative and positive.
since it is simply to affirm
something we believe.

What we will see here for the next 31 days are simple affirmations allowing you to become the observer of your mental space and the beliefs you have.

Take the time to be aware of your breathing and your energy when you start a day. Take the time to breathe in deeply and breathe out with a smile before you start saying and repeating the affirmation of the day. Take the time to set your intention, which is to simply feel better.

Take time to feel what you are saying or take time to repeat until you feel what is said.

Take the time…to take the time is the key.

It doesn't matter if you spend two minutes or fifteen minutes, and if you listen to meditation music at the same time or not, as long as you take the time to feel its power, the power to connect to your great and divine potential.

Each day you will find a new affirmation and a few questions helping your mindfulness journey, and helping you better reprogram your personal database, your subconscious.

Enjoy your mindfulness journey!

*Nothing is complicated,
everything is simple,
yet simplicity
is complicated for the ego.*

Day 1

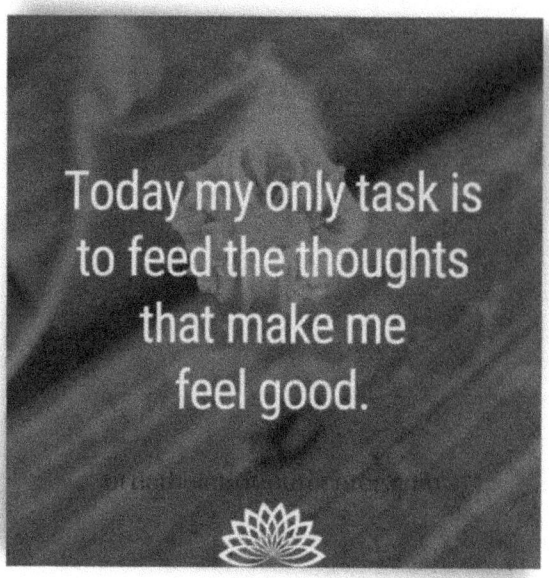

Now take the time to read and repeat it until you feel good and in tune. You are doing this for no one but yourself, so take the time and enjoy believing in your magnificent power within.

What was my first ego-based thought reaction when I read it? (Be mindful of your journey.)

How will I remember today to stop feeding the negative thoughts? (Be aware and trust.)

Can I commit to being proud of myself no matter the result, simply because I am mindful of my own journey and the beautiful Me that I am already? (Allow your Inner Self to shine.)

I invite you to come back to the affirmation at the end of your day. What did you observe about today's affirmation?

Day 2

Now take the time to read and repeat it until you feel good and in tune. You are doing this for no one but yourself, so take the time and enjoy believing in your magnificent power within.

What was my first ego-based thought reaction when I read it? (Be mindful of your journey.)

How will I remember today to feel good before I take any action or say something? (Be aware and trust.)

Can I commit to being proud of myself no matter the result, simply because I am mindful of my own journey and the beautiful Me that I am already? (Allow your Inner Self to shine.)

I invite you to come back to the affirmation at the end of your day. What did you observe about today's affirmation?

Day 3

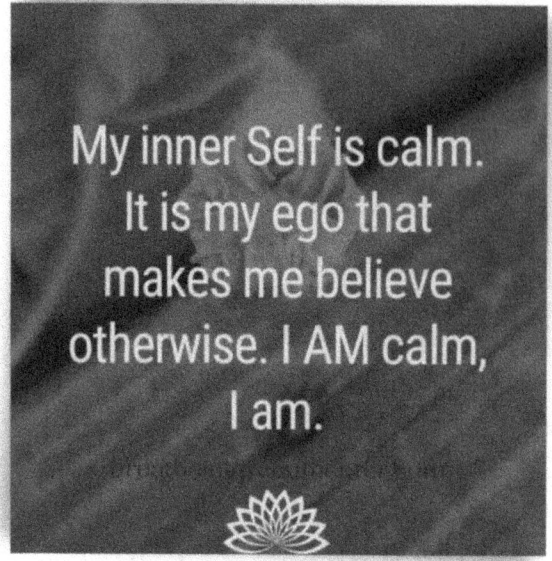

Now take the time to read and repeat it until you feel good and in tune. You are doing this for no one but yourself, so take the time and enjoy believing in your magnificent power within.

What was my first ego-based thought reaction when I read it? (Be mindful of your journey.)

How will I remember today... to remember that it is my ego that is not calm? (Be aware and trust.)

Can I commit to being proud of myself no matter the result, simply because I am mindful of my own journey and the beautiful Me that I am already? (Allow your Inner Self to shine.)

I invite you to come back to the affirmation at the end of your day. What did you observe about today's affirmation?

Day 4

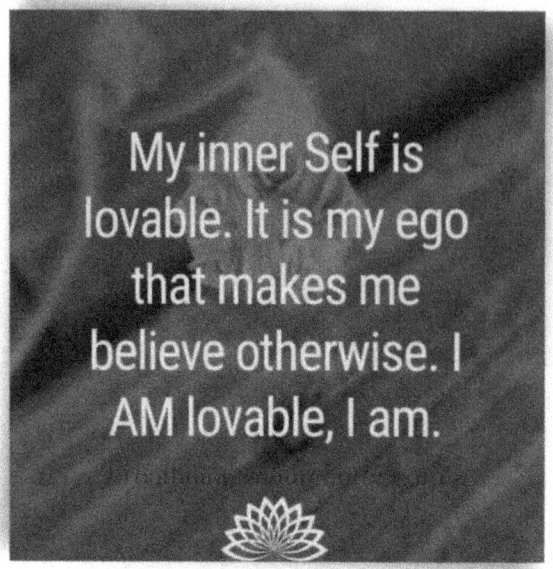

Now take the time to read and repeat it until you feel good and in tune. You are doing this for no one but yourself, so take the time and enjoy believing in your magnificent power within.

What was my first ego-based thought reaction when I read it? (Be mindful of your journey.)

How will I remember today... that I am lovable despite what my ego makes me believe about myself? (Be aware and trust.)

Can I commit to being proud of myself no matter the result, simply because I am mindful of my own journey and the beautiful Me that I am already? (Allow your Inner Self to shine.)

I invite you to come back to the affirmation at the end of your day. What did you observe about today's affirmation?

Day 5

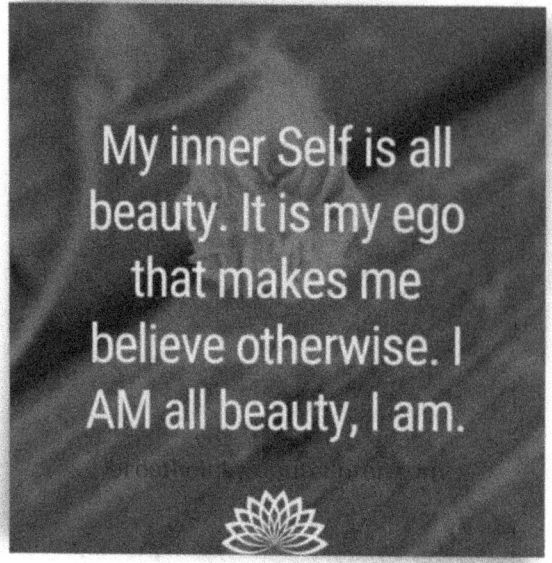

Now take the time to read and repeat it until you feel good and in tune. You are doing this for no one but yourself, so take the time and enjoy believing in your magnificent power within.

What was my first ego-based thought reaction when I read it? (Be mindful of your journey.)

How will I remember today... that I am pure beauty, I am beauty-full, despite what my ego makes me believe about myself? (Be aware and trust.)

Can I commit to being proud of myself no matter the result, simply because I am mindful of my own journey and the beautiful Me that I am already? (Allow your Inner Self to shine.)

I invite you to come back to the affirmation at the end of your day. What did you observe about today's affirmation?

Day 6

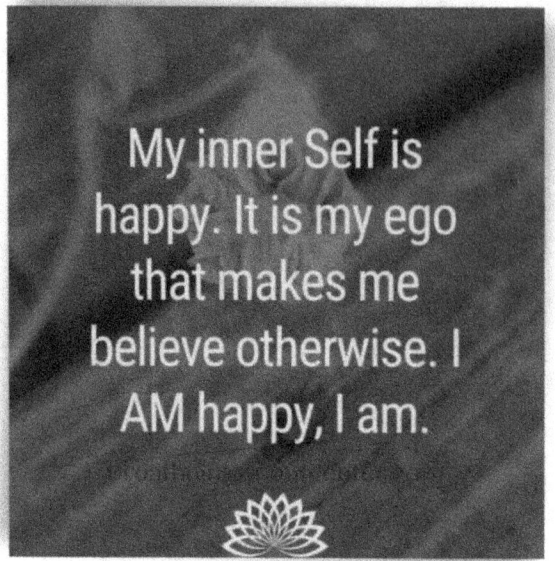

Now take the time to read and repeat it until you feel good and in tune. You are doing this for no one but yourself, so take the time and enjoy believing in your magnificent power within.

What was my first ego-based thought reaction when I read it? (Be mindful of your journey.)

How will I remember today... that I am a happy person, and that it is my ego that generates expectations? (Be aware and trust.)

Can I commit to being proud of myself no matter the result, simply because I am mindful of my own journey and the beautiful Me that I am already? (Allow your Inner Self to shine.)

I invite you to come back to the affirmation at the end of your day. What did you observe about today's affirmation?

Day 7

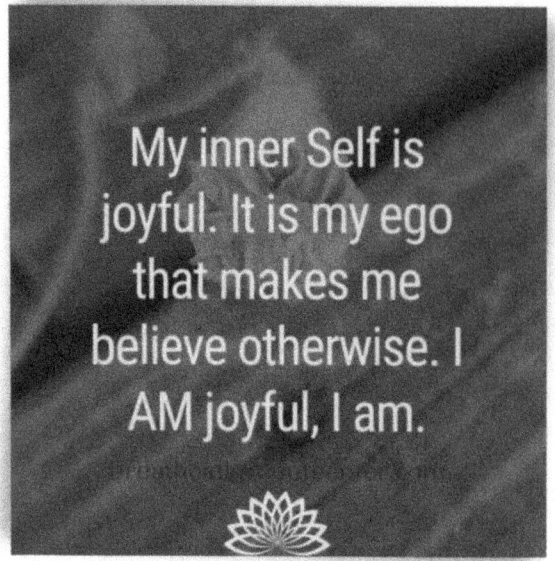

Now take the time to read and repeat it until you feel good and in tune. You are doing this for no one but yourself, so take the time and enjoy believing in your magnificent power within.

What was my first ego-based thought reaction when I read it? (Be mindful of your journey.)

How will I remember today… that I am a joyful person, despite my ego-based thoughts and perceptions? (Be aware and trust.)

Can I commit to being proud of myself no matter the result, simply because I am mindful of my own journey and the beautiful Me that I am already? (Allow your Inner Self to shine.)

I invite you to come back to the affirmation at the end of your day. What did you observe about today's affirmation?

Day 8

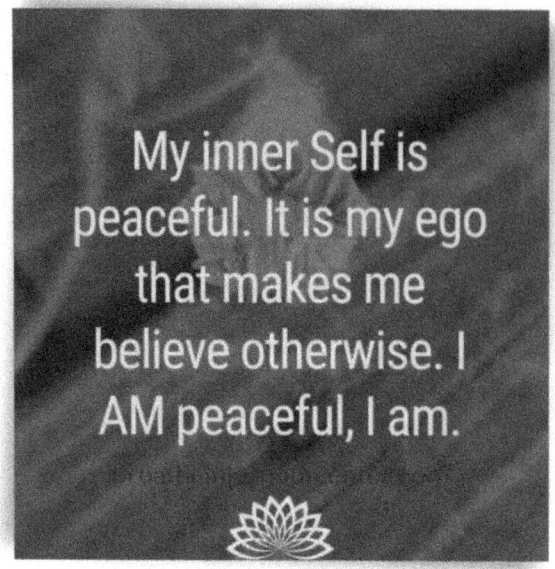

Now take the time to read and repeat it until you feel good and in tune. You are doing this for no one but yourself, so take the time and enjoy believing in your magnificent power within.

What was my first ego-based thought reaction when I read it? (Be mindful of your journey.)

How will I remember today... that I am a peaceful person, despite what my ego-based mind triggers, it is my ego's reactions not my True Self? (Be aware and trust.)

Can I commit to being proud of myself no matter the result, simply because I am mindful of my own journey and the beautiful Me that I am already? (Allow your Inner Self to shine.)

I invite you to come back to the affirmation at the end of your day. What did you observe about today's affirmation?

Day 9

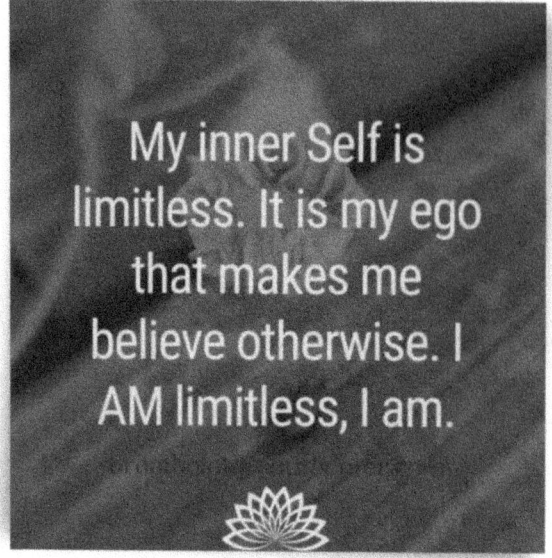

Now take the time to read and repeat it until you feel good and in tune. You are doing this for no one but yourself, so take the time and enjoy believing in your magnificent power within.

What was my first ego-based thought reaction when I read it? (Be mindful of your journey.)

How will I remember today... that all my limitations and limited beliefs are from my ego-based mind keeping me from moving outside "a" comfort zone, an ego-comfort zone? (Be aware and trust.)

Can I commit to being proud of myself no matter the result, simply because I am mindful of my own journey and the beautiful Me that I am already? (Allow your Inner Self to shine.)

I invite you to come back to the affirmation at the end of your day. What did you observe about today's affirmation?

Day 10

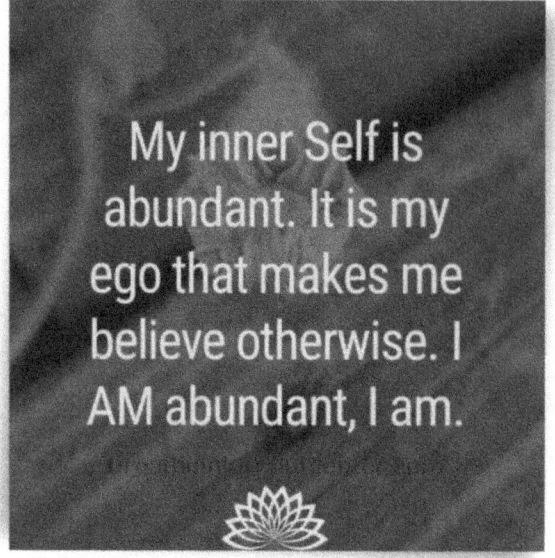

Now take the time to read and repeat it until you feel good and in tune. You are doing this for no one but yourself, so take the time and enjoy believing in your magnificent power within.

What was my first ego-based thought reaction when I read it? (Be mindful of your journey.)

How will I remember today… that I am living in abundance, and that my ego-based mind perception is not the one to define what abundance is nor when it is?

I have everything I need every morning, either already material and manifested or the idea and means to get what I will be needing. (Be aware and trust.)

Can I commit to being proud of myself no matter the result, simply because I am mindful of my own journey and the beautiful Me that I am already? (Allow your Inner Self to shine.)

I invite you to come back to the affirmation at the end of your day. What did you observe about today's affirmation?

Day 11

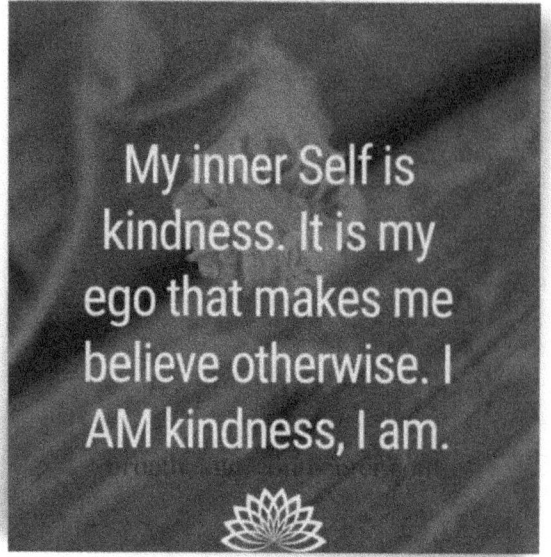

Now take the time to read and repeat it until you feel good and in tune. You are doing this for no one but yourself, so take the time and enjoy believing in your magnificent power within.

What was my first ego-based thought reaction when I read it? (Be mindful of your journey.)

How will I remember today... that I am a kind person and that when I am not, I am under the influence of my ego-based mind.
(Be aware and trust.)

Can I commit to being proud of myself no matter the result, simply because I am mindful of my own journey and the beautiful Me that I am already? (Allow your Inner Self to shine.)

I invite you to come back to the affirmation at the end of your day. What did you observe about today's affirmation?

Day 12

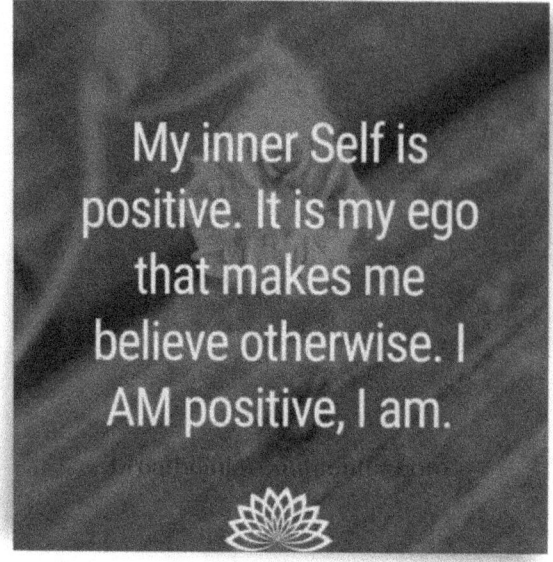

Now take the time to read and repeat it until you feel good and in tune. You are doing this for no one but yourself, so take the time and enjoy believing in your magnificent power within.

What was my first ego-based thought reaction when I read it? (Be mindful of your journey.)

How will I remember today... that I am a positive being experiencing life and all that I can do and be, and that when I am not, I am under the influence of my ego-based mind. (Be aware and trust.)

Can I commit to being proud of myself no matter the result, simply because I am mindful of my own journey and the beautiful Me that I am already? (Allow your Inner Self to shine.)

I invite you to come back to the affirmation at the end of your day. What did you observe about today's affirmation?

Day 13

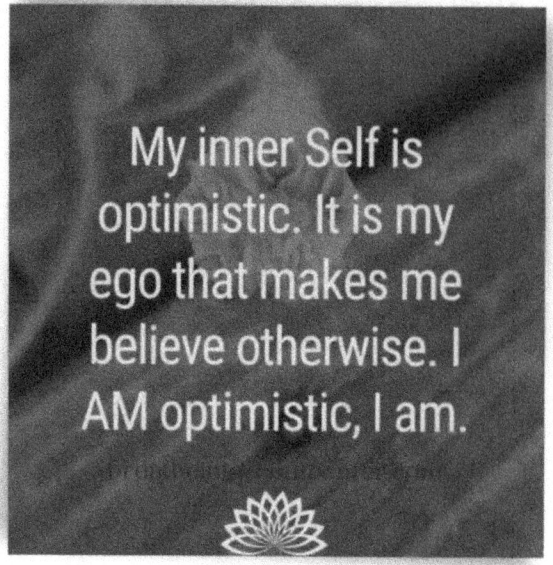

Now take the time to read and repeat it until you feel good and in tune. You are doing this for no one but yourself, so take the time and enjoy believing in your magnificent power within.

What was my first ego-based thought reaction when I read it? (Be mindful of your journey.)

How will I remember today... that I can see the positive side of everything, and that I am the one creating the stories in my mind. I can imagine = image in... the way I choose. I feed the story I choose to feed. (Be aware and trust.)

Can I commit to being proud of myself no matter the result, simply because I am mindful of my own journey and the beautiful Me that I am already? (Allow your Inner Self to shine.)

I invite you to come back to the affirmation at the end of your day. What did you observe about today's affirmation?

Day 14

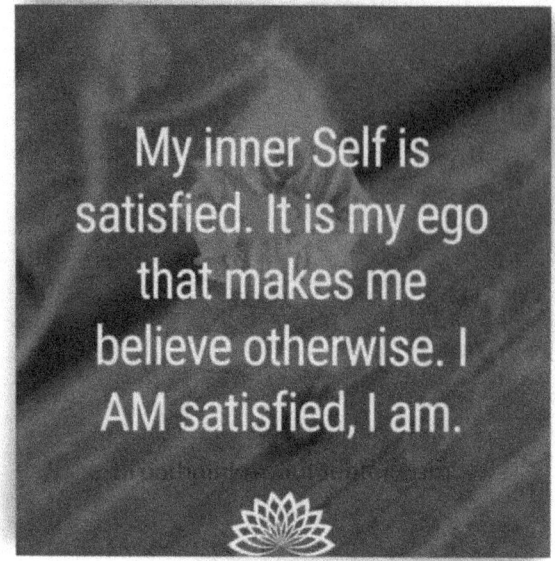

Now take the time to read and repeat it until you feel good and in tune. You are doing this for no one but yourself, so take the time and enjoy believing in your magnificent power within.

What was my first ego-based thought reaction when I read it? (Be mindful of your journey.)

How will I remember today... that I can be Soul satisfied and not ego-satisfied? Only the ego is conditionally satisfied. (Be aware and trust.)

Can I commit to being proud of myself no matter the result, simply because I am mindful of my own journey and the beautiful Me that I am already? (Allow your Inner Self to shine.)

I invite you to come back to the affirmation at the end of your day. What did you observe about today's affirmation?

Day 15

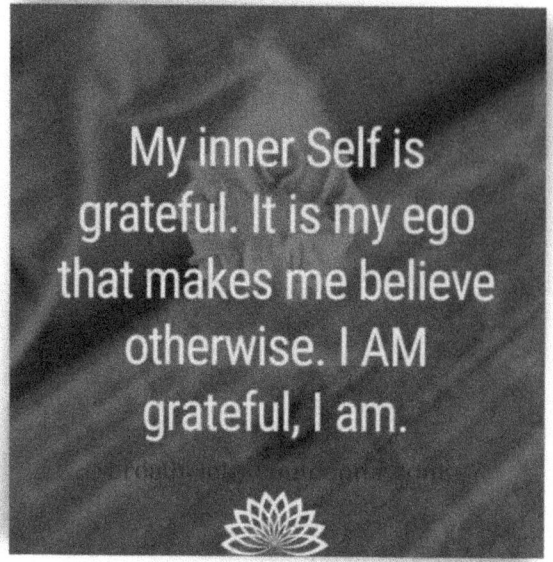

Now take the time to read and repeat it until you feel good and in tune. You are doing this for no one but yourself, so take the time and enjoy believing in your magnificent power within.

What was my first ego-based thought reaction when I read it? (Be mindful of your journey.)

How will I remember today... that I can be grateful for many things even for the negativity allowing leap of faith or inspired actions or Inner courage? Only the ego is conditionally grateful. (Be aware and trust.)

Can I commit to being proud of myself no matter the result, simply because I am mindful of my own journey and the beautiful Me that I am already? (Allow your Inner Self to shine.)

I invite you to come back to the affirmation at the end of your day. What did you observe about today's affirmation?

Day 16

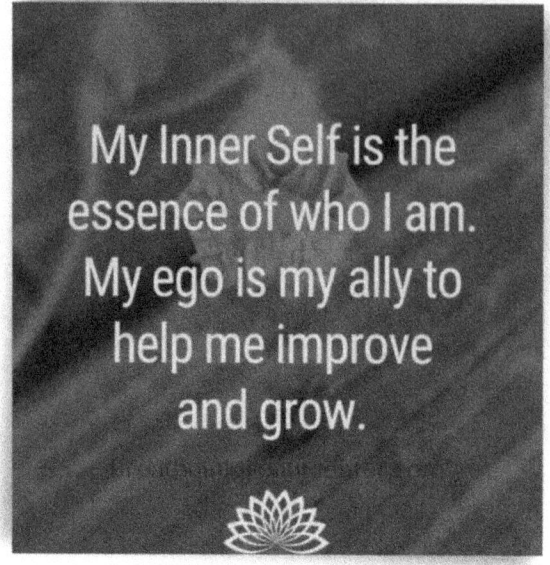

Now take the time to read and repeat it until you feel good and in tune. You are doing this for no one but yourself, so take the time and enjoy believing in your magnificent power within.

What was my first ego-based thought reaction when I read it? (Be mindful of your journey.)

How will I remember today... that in my heart I know exactly who I am and how wonderful I am and how perfect I am. My essence is purely divine. I AM that, I am. I am experiencing all that I can be and become. I am learning and expanding through my life experiences and expressions. My ego is my ally showing me what is misaligned with my True Self, when I am misaligned with my True Self and my essence, through negative emotions and negative feelings and negative perceptions. (Be aware and trust.)

Can I commit to being proud of myself no matter the result, simply because I am mindful of my own journey and the beautiful Me that I am already? (Allow your Inner Self to shine.)

I invite you to come back to the affirmation at the end of your day. What did you observe about today's affirmation?

Day 17

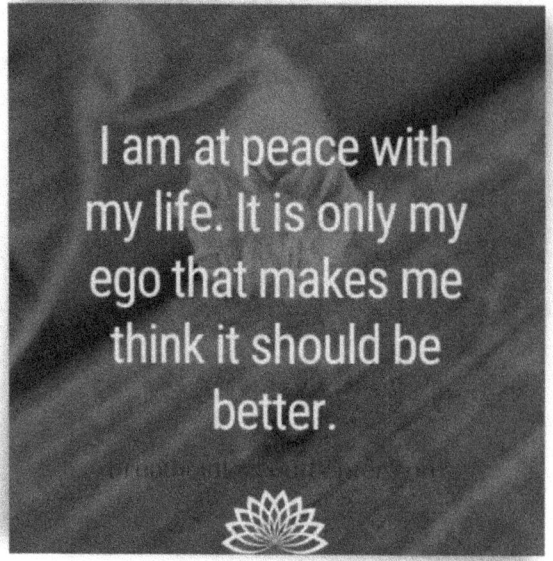

Now take the time to read and repeat it until you feel good and in tune. You are doing this for no one but yourself, so take the time and enjoy believing in your magnificent power within.

What was my first ego-based thought reaction when I read it? (Be mindful of your journey.)

How am I going to remember today...that where I am today...I once desired it, and sometimes it's disguised in the details that I forgot, that I have you ever asked? Maybe I thought of a different how, a how from my ego. Only my ego can make me believe that my life "should" be better, not allowing me to be at peace with my life in its present moment.

I am on a personal journey, and I will never arrive at my ego's destination because the ego is never happy or satisfied. I am in the right place at the right time somewhere on my evolutionary cycle of what is.

When it's not satisfying in any way, it just serves as a steppingstone out of my ego-comfort zone, (trusting my inner wings) so I am always in the right place at the right time.

...sometimes certain components need to be ready for me before I arrive. How am I going to remember today that I can be at peace with my life? (Be aware and trust.)

Can I commit to being proud of myself no matter the result, simply because I am mindful of my own journey and the beautiful Me that I am already? (Allow your Inner Self to shine.)

I invite you to come back to the affirmation at the end of your day. What did you observe about today's affirmation?

Breathe In,
let go of your ego-based thoughts and vision,
see from your Soul,
and **Love Out!**

Day 18

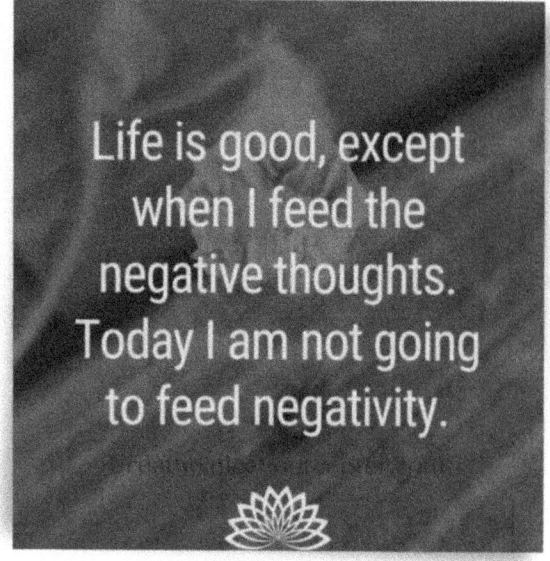

Now take the time to read and repeat it until you feel good and in tune. You are doing this for no one but yourself, so take the time and enjoy believing in your magnificent power within.

What was my first ego-based thought reaction when I read it? (Be mindful of your journey.)

How am I going to remember today...not to feed negative thoughts, tempting and easy as it may be at times?

It is my choice to feed the story that I want to nurture in my mind, in my mental space. It is my choice to feed the negativity allowing the negative story to grow and grow like a snowball. It is also my choice to do something else to keep my mind busy with something else, even if it is just washing my hands.

I can see that life is beautiful if I choose to see that it is. (Be aware and trust.)

Can I commit to being proud of myself no matter the result, simply because I am mindful of my own journey and the beautiful Me that I am already? (Allow your Inner Self to shine.)

I invite you to come back to the affirmation at the end of your day. What did you observe about today's affirmation?

Day 19

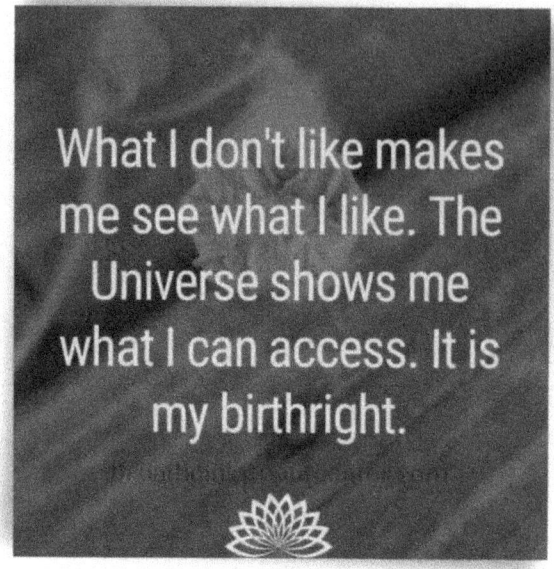

Now take the time to read and repeat it until you feel good and in tune. You are doing this for no one but yourself, so take the time and enjoy believing in your magnificent power within.

What was my first ego-based thought reaction when I read it? (Be mindful of your journey.)

How am I going to remember today... to see the other side of what I do not love... to name and claim what I love instead that comes from my heart?

It is often by knowing what I don't want that I can clarify what I want, and the Universe helps me see it from my heart.

How am I going to remember today to happily focus on what I want and leave no mental space or heart for what I don't want? (Be aware and trust.)

Can I commit to being proud of myself no matter the result, simply because I am mindful of my own journey and the beautiful Me that I am already? (Allow your Inner Self to shine.)

I invite you to come back to the affirmation at the end of your day. What did you observe about today's affirmation?

Day 20

Now take the time to read and repeat it until you feel good and in tune. You are doing this for no one but yourself, so take the time and enjoy believing in your magnificent power within.

What was my first ego-based thought reaction when I read it? (Be mindful of your journey.)

How am I going to remember today...to remember that the unknown is unknown only to my ego which cannot access the unseen but only the active data in my database, my subconscious (my past and my unchanged beliefs)? Trust or faith is trusting my intuition, my inspirations, and my inspired actions even if I do not yet see the next step which may only unfold once I get there. (Be aware and trust.)

Can I commit to being proud of myself no matter the result, simply because I am mindful of my own journey and the beautiful Me that I am already? (Allow your Inner Self to shine.)

I invite you to come back to the affirmation at the end of your day. What did you observe about today's affirmation?

Day 21

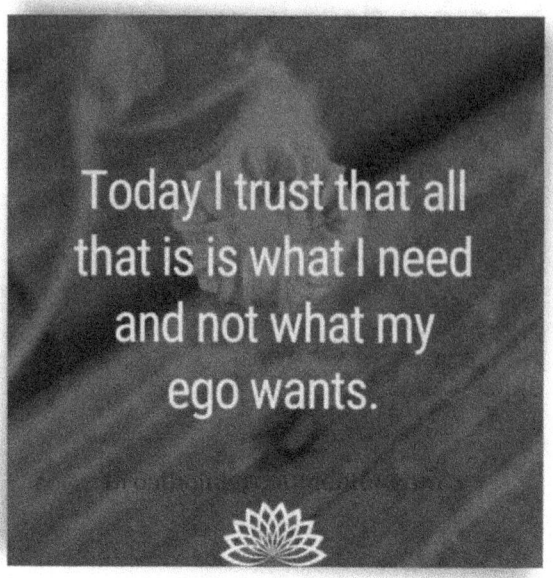

Now take the time to read and repeat it until you feel good and in tune. You are doing this for no one but yourself, so take the time and enjoy believing in your magnificent power within.

What was my first ego-based thought reaction when I read it? (Be mindful of your journey.)

How am I going to remember today... that all there is... is what I need now? And yes, I can desire more, but everything I need for any reason is already in my now and it's up to me to see it without my perception coming from my ego.

Only my ego will make me believe that I am missing something or someone different in order to improve myself throughout my journey. My inner Self can guide me. (Be aware and trust.)

Can I commit to being proud of myself no matter the result, simply because I am mindful of my own journey and the beautiful Me that I am already? (Allow your Inner Self to shine.)

I invite you to come back to the affirmation at the end of your day. What did you observe about today's affirmation?

Day 22

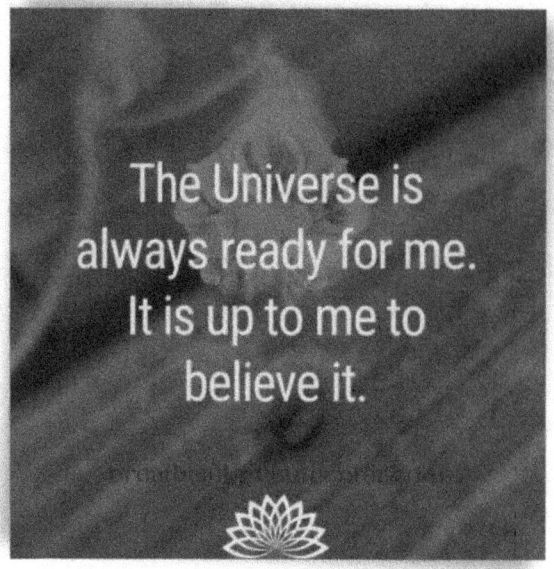

Now take the time to read and repeat it until you feel good and in tune. You are doing this for no one but yourself, so take the time and enjoy believing in your magnificent power within.

What was my first ego-based thought reaction when I read it? (Be mindful of your journey.)

How am I going to remember today... that I have every right to ask the Universe (or God, or Source or Infinite Intelligence, whatever you call it to feel comfortable)? The Universe is always ready for me, for my requests no matter how many...the ones that come from my heart and not from my ego (which often explains why people stop believing that their requests are heard because those of the ego are not real demands or desires). (Be aware and trust.)

Can I commit to being proud of myself no matter the result, simply because I am mindful of my own journey and the beautiful Me that I am already? (Allow your Inner Self to shine.)

I invite you to come back to the affirmation at the end of your day. What did you observe about today's affirmation?

Day 23

Now take the time to read and repeat it until you feel good and in tune. You are doing this for no one but yourself, so take the time and enjoy believing in your magnificent power within.

What was my first ego-based thought reaction when I read it? (Be mindful of your journey.)

How am I going to remember today... that the Source of the Universe is my main source of supply? My ego can show me ways through thoughts and ideas that make me think I have to find ways to get this or that "on my own", but my main source of supply can be reached from within myself and contains an infinite supply and means that my ego cannot see (yet). (Be aware and trust.)

Can I commit to being proud of myself no matter the result, simply because I am mindful of my own journey and the beautiful Me that I am already? (Allow your Inner Self to shine.)

I invite you to come back to the affirmation at the end of your day. What did you observe about today's affirmation?

Day 24

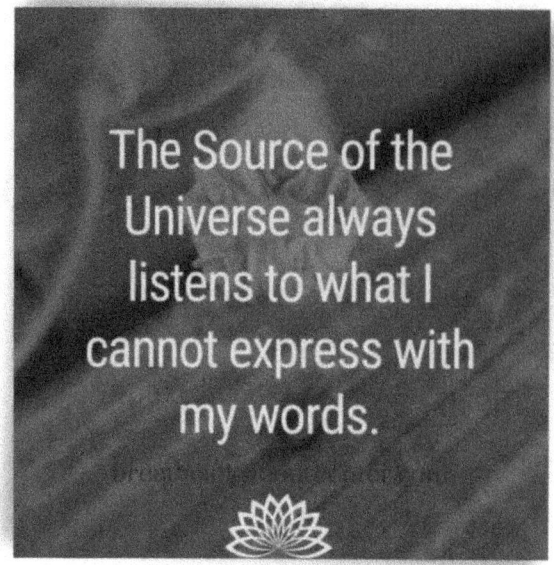

Now take the time to read and repeat it until you feel good and in tune. You are doing this for no one but yourself, so take the time and enjoy believing in your magnificent power within.

What was my first ego-based thought reaction when I read it? (Be mindful of your journey.)

How will I remember today... that Source (or God or Infinite Intelligence whichever you prefer and feel comfortable with) listens and will always listen... even and especially when I don't use words. My tears, my sighs, my deepest feelings, and the desires of my heart are all heard. Source includes all that I cannot express. (Be aware and trust.)

Can I commit to being proud of myself no matter the result, simply because I am mindful of my own journey and the beautiful Me that I am already? (Allow your Inner Self to shine.)

I invite you to come back to the affirmation at the end of your day. What did you observe about today's affirmation?

Day 25

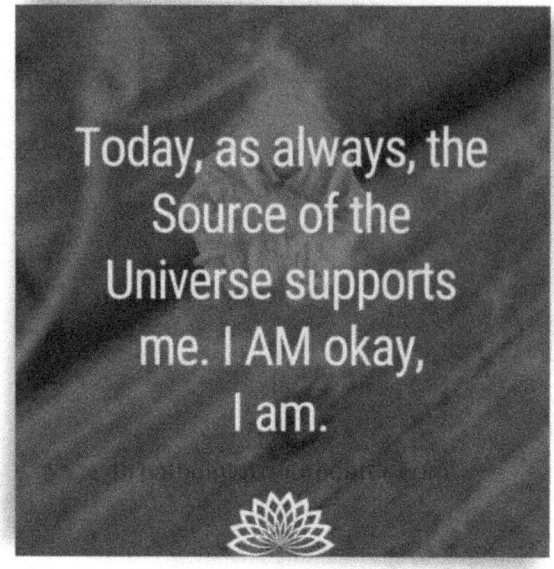

Now take the time to read and repeat it until you feel good and in tune. You are doing this for no one but yourself, so take the time and enjoy believing in your magnificent power within.

What was my first ego-based thought reaction when I read it? (Be mindful of your journey.)

How am I going to remember today...that my ego might make me feel like I am alone in life and situations, when I am not? I am fully supported, and my ego prefers to show me the "support I don't have" instead of the support I have, including that of my powerful inner Self. (Be aware and trust.)

Can I commit to being proud of myself no matter the result, simply because I am mindful of my own journey and the beautiful Me that I am already? (Allow your Inner Self to shine.)

I invite you to come back to the affirmation at the end of your day. What did you observe about today's affirmation?

Day 26

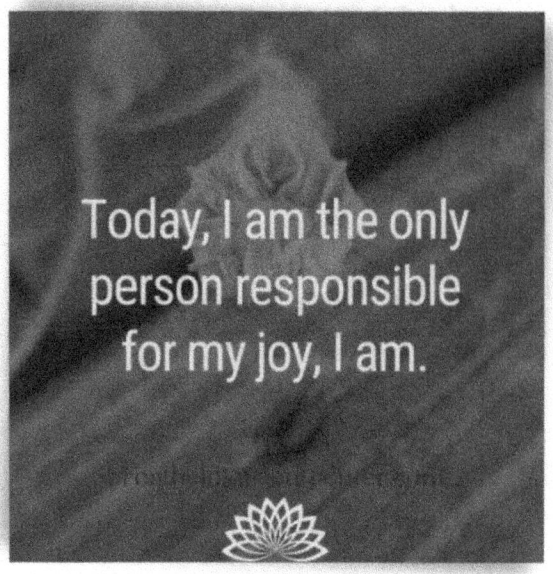

Now take the time to read and repeat it until you feel good and in tune. You are doing this for no one but yourself, so take the time and enjoy believing in your magnificent power within.

What was my first ego-based thought reaction when I read it? (Be mindful of your journey.)

How am I going to remember today... that my joy is unconditional? No one is responsible for my joy. I am responsible for what I see and how I choose to see, react, feel and be. Only my ego makes joy conditional on external manifestations. I have this power in Me! (Be aware and trust.)

Can I commit to being proud of myself no matter the result, simply because I am mindful of my own journey and the beautiful Me that I am already? (Allow your Inner Self to shine.)

I invite you to come back to the affirmation at the end of your day. What did you observe about today's affirmation?

Day 27

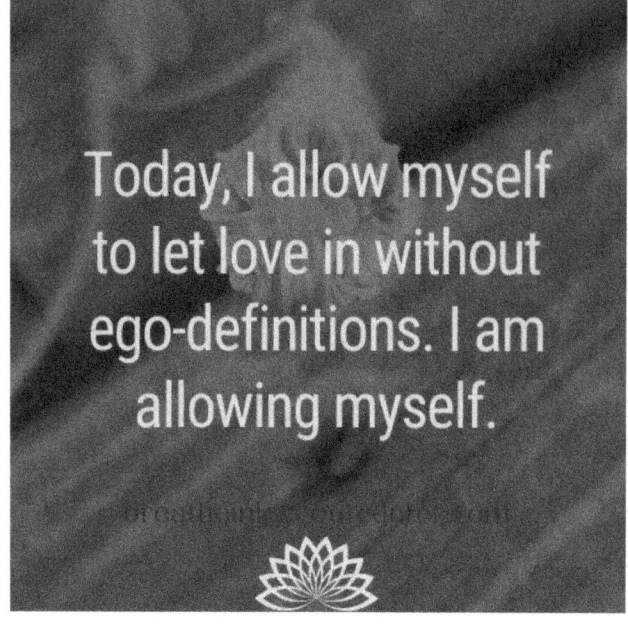

Now take the time to read and repeat it until you feel good and in tune. You are doing this for no one but yourself, so take the time and enjoy believing in your magnificent power within.

What was my first ego-based thought reaction when I read it? (Be mindful of your journey.)

How am I going to remember today... to allow love to be love without my ego-definitions or the expectations I already have of what love is and what it is not? Love is kind. Love has no expectations. Love is simple. Love is everywhere and in everything and everyone; and it is my task to see it beyond the limits of my ego. I get more love than my ego lets me see. (Be aware and trust.)

Can I commit to being proud of myself no matter the result, simply because I am mindful of my own journey and the beautiful Me that I am already? (Allow your Inner Self to shine.)

I invite you to come back to the affirmation at the end of your day. What did you observe about today's affirmation?

Day 28

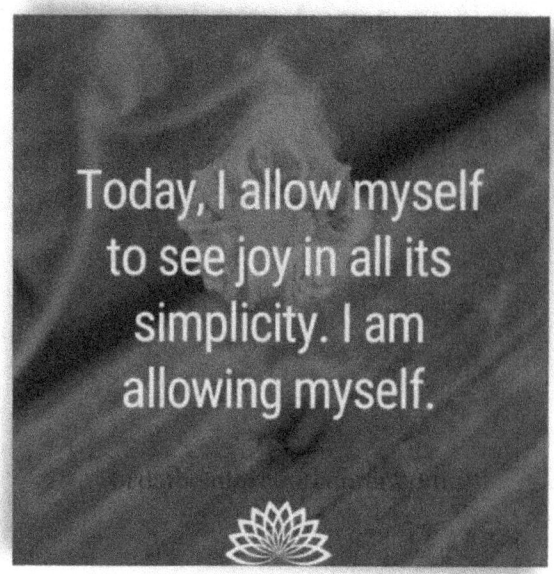

Now take the time to read and repeat it until you feel good and in tune. You are doing this for no one but yourself, so take the time and enjoy believing in your magnificent power within.

What was my first ego-based thought reaction when I read it? (Be mindful of your journey.)

How am I going to remember today... to see joy through the eyes of a child? It is present everywhere and I can adjust my focus to see it. (Be aware and trust.)

Can I commit to being proud of myself no matter the result, simply because I am mindful of my own journey and the beautiful Me that I am already? (Allow your Inner Self to shine.)

I invite you to come back to the affirmation at the end of your day. What did you observe about today's affirmation?

Day 29

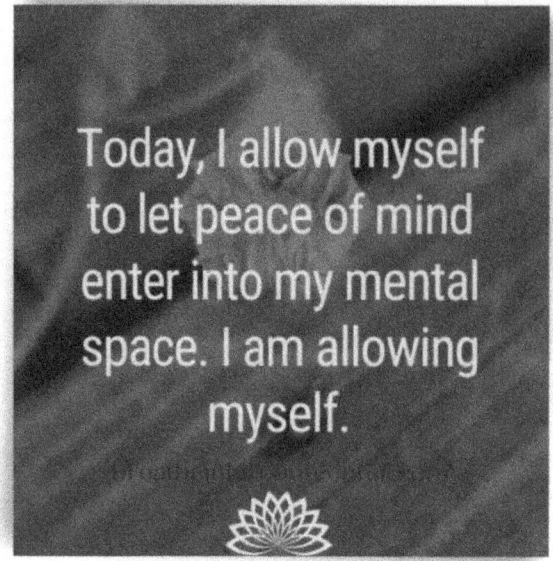

Now take the time to read and repeat it until you feel good and in tune. You are doing this for no one but yourself, so take the time and enjoy believing in your magnificent power within.

What was my first ego-based thought reaction when I read it? (Be mindful of your journey.)

How am I going to remember today... to stop feeding the negative; to inspire, to love and to smile more, and to allow peace of mind to be? (Be aware and trust.)

Can I commit to being proud of myself no matter the result, simply because I am mindful of my own journey and the beautiful Me that I am already? (Allow your Inner Self to shine.)

I invite you to come back to the affirmation at the end of your day. What did you observe about today's affirmation?

Day 30

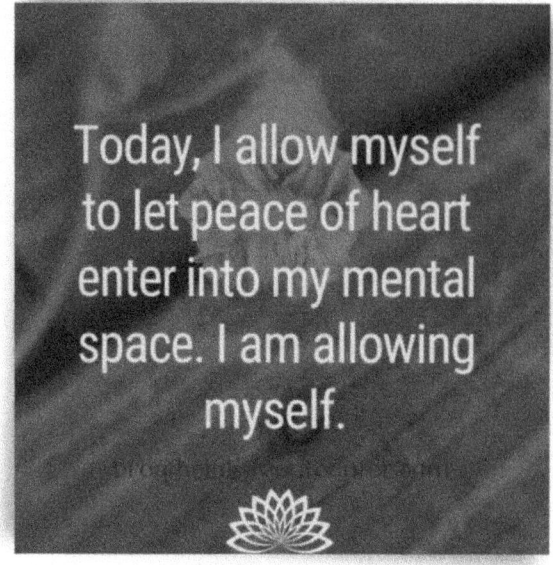

Now take the time to read and repeat it until you feel good and in tune. You are doing this for no one but yourself, so take the time and enjoy believing in your magnificent power within.

What was my first ego-based thought reaction when I read it? (Be mindful of your journey.)

How am I going to remember today… to stop judging situations and people including myself? Only my ego makes me believe with *should have been/do, must be/do, should be/do* **differently than it was and is and will be.**

How am I going to remember today to see that today is, and tomorrow will become the new "today is"?

Peace of heart creates peace of mind. I am powerful enough to create my own peace of heart. (Be aware and trust.)

Can I commit to being proud of myself no matter the result, simply because I am mindful of my own journey and the beautiful Me that I am already? (Allow your Inner Self to shine.)

I invite you to come back to the affirmation at the end of your day. What did you observe about today's affirmation?

Day 31

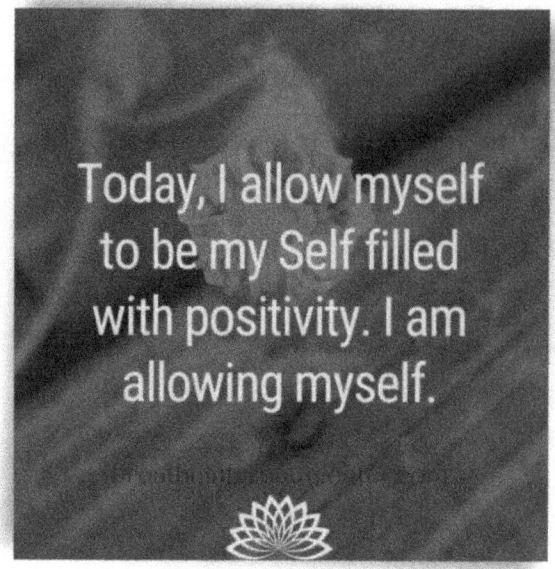

Now take the time to read and repeat it until you feel good and in tune. You are doing this for no one but yourself, so take the time and enjoy believing in your magnificent power within.

What was my first ego-based thought reaction when I read it? (Be mindful of your journey.)

How am I going to remember today that my inner Self is me, my True Self of pure positivity, and that I am living and enjoying this wonderful journey of all that I can be and become? I am a spiritual being and a physical being. I am a spiritual being who experiences life through my physical being and not the other way around. It is my task to allow my inner Self to shine. (Be aware and trust.)

Can I commit to being proud of myself no matter the result, simply because I am mindful of my own journey and the beautiful Me that I am already? (Allow your Inner Self to shine.)

I invite you to come back to the affirmation at the end of your day. What did you observe about today's affirmation?

Do you know what you just finished?

You have just given yourself new beliefs to write your story, the one you want to write.

You have taken the time to **better understand when your ego is in action** in your mental space.

You have had a wonderful mindfulness journey, or even spiritual awakening regardless of which path you have taken. Congratulations on having done this work of deepening your consciousness, of your wonderful infinite power that you already have within you. You are already declaring the changes you want to experience effortlessly.

The goal was to learn how to better connect to your Self without triggering your ego to accept new concepts about yourself, about your Self. And this is just the beginning of a wonderful adventure.

Although I am an expert in this matter, I still have to remind myself of this infinite divine source of supply and this infinite divine power which is also mine, because I am a spiritual being who experiences life expanding my Self and expanding the Universe by co-creating all that exists.

On any life journey, the ego being part of our everything interferes here and there, so it's up to us to take the time... to take the time to remember who we really are, our Authentic Self.

I decided to publish a revised edition because while working on another book, I realized that certain passages could add a lot of value here. A few things were added here and there at the very beginning and now I would like to share something with you that might help you deepen the concept of wholeness of the magnificent person that you are.

Life is simple, it is the ego that complicates it.

~~me, myself, i~~ ME, myself, I

Throughout our lives, we transform, without necessarily being aware of it while we are doing it, because we transform by default. That's what you're doing here.

Then comes a day when you become fully aware that not only are you changing, but you can help yourself create your reality. We can be co-creators of our life and our tomorrow. We have our say. After all, it's our life! It is often this part of co-creation that requires a little help and guidance, or a lot of clarity at the risk of creating from one's ego-desires.

Like a caterpillar that becomes a butterfly, we feel and feel a change in progress or a need for change because we understand that what we were until now has had its day. We do not always know why, but we know that an energy of change lives within us.

We understand that we transform, that we change, that we evolve. We make choices that are sometimes conscious and perhaps less and less often unconscious. We sometimes make choices that do not give the results we thought we were experiencing simply because these choices were suggested by our ego.

It doesn't matter if our choices come from our ego or from our Inner Self (or Higher Self), we know that we are transforming. Although we know that we are going through a change, and that we know that we are no longer the person we were before, we do not understand anything at the same time because nothing is going right. We have lost our landmarks.

We feel that our old selves are dying, but we don't yet know what will become of us. We do not know that we are opening up to our Self, with a capital M. We do not know that we are gradually leaving aside our ego-identity, I am, and that we are opening up to our inner Self, I am, bringing different perceptions of everything around us and what we experience. We begin to see from our inner Self.

What seemed true is false, and what seemed false may still be false. What's left? What was known is no longer known and the ego has no access to the unknown. And here, fear can inhabit us. The fear of change. The ego uses uncertainty to generate an emotion of fear.

We can feel that we are taking an unknown path, strewn with strangers. And the ego does not like the unknown, because the ego cannot see the unknown and does not have access to the unknown, only to the database with the already recorded data of past experiences and past emotions. Quite simply. The ego cannot draw its new information from our personal database, our subconscious, because we are creating it with our inner Self. The ego only exists in its world of illusions. Self-identity is changing.

On this path strewn with unknowns, we have new values, new beliefs, new skills and new knowledge, but we don't even know how to use them or perhaps what some will be used for. We don't see tomorrow the same way because we create it now with known data and unknown data from our ego and its thought system, and a little less by default. Our old settings are no longer accurate.

There can be a lot of confusion in our mental space. We can no longer fight to return to what we were before. The call of evolution is bigger and stronger than the past. The security of knowing who we were and simply following old patterns keeping us in an ego-comfort zone is also very present, but nothing is right.

We can even be afraid of dying. The ego that does not want to lose its control associates having less control with its destruction. And, since we have associated ourselves for perhaps our entire lives with believing that we are our ego, this fear seems real. We can also fight mentally not to change because the ego believes that its end is near.

And the ego belongs to the physical body so it emits a false belief that it may be time to end its life or that its end is approaching. The only end that is near is the end of ego control which will have to take its place in the passenger seat.

Then we go back to the obvious. The one we know we can never back down from. We evolve. We accept our evolution. Life moves forward. So we give up. We abandon the fight of non-change. We surrender to greater than ourselves, to novelty and to what we are becoming. We may think that we are falling, but we are not falling, we are simply falling within ourselves. We get closer to the Self or the inner Me who knows exactly that life is beautiful and positive.

The caterpillar is becoming a butterfly. The desire for release is bigger than the little me trying to hold back the change.

When a caterpillar becomes a butterfly, its state of being unravels, becomes sticky and deformed because it is no longer what it was, and it is not yet quite what it will become. She transforms.

Something similar happens with our state of being for some time. There is a distortion of our system of thoughts. Like a bad amalgamation of two opposing thought systems. This transformation will not cause us to change our thought system completely, but it will allow us to understand what we were and what we are now, and to accept our full potential to become even more in stopping to believe that our ego is who we are with its limiting ideas.

After accepting the change and evolution of our inner state of being, we begin to look forward to seeing what we will become. We're starting to appreciate our new colors and our new abilities that we haven't tried yet, but we can understand, we know, that it will be great.

On our evolutionary journey, we open our wings and see our life from a new angle. We see the world from a new angle with new perceptions. Our ego-identity has changed. Although these are often ego-perceptions, sometimes we can see with a big picture, and often all the pieces that come together and take shape make sense because we no longer see them separately, but we see that everything makes a whole. We see that everything is perfect. We understand that everything had its place and purpose, including our ego, including all our experiences because everything is part of a whole and we are that whole. We understand the I am even if some things will require a little more clarification.

We are used to seeing the physical body grow and evolve in age from birth to physical death, but we are less used to seeing the evolution of our inner journey. This is called an awakening of consciousness, when we realize that we are much more than the physical body and the brain that we think we know. In fact, we are only remembering who we are, the essence of our being that was to become. The more we evolve, the more or forget who we are to remember who we are.

We go from "I, me, me" to "I, me, Me" through a panoply of healing old beliefs, that is, by stopping believing in our old ego-beliefs. But before arriving at this awakening of consciousness and this deeper state of being, there is a whole world to understand. There are new perceptions, new definitions, new beliefs to integrate to put the ego in the passenger seat, which is a natural step to take.

When we open our wings, we learn to live and love to live with our new attributes, our new skills and our new perceptions. There's a whole new world to explore. Our reality has changed. And casually, our reality can change from day to day because we still go from one ego-identity to another.

Sometimes, when we look in detail, we can recall an event, or an element of life before. If or when we forget what we have become because we choose to visit a detail any longer, we may even find ourselves unable to see the big picture or fly with our new self. As if having a broken wing makes us believe that we can no longer fly or makes us see only a small part of a whole... like before we knew how to fly.

We can find ourselves taking one small step at a time with the fear of dying because we think that if we can no longer fly with our wings, we will die on the way to nowhere. The ego tries to regain control. And when the destinations and objectives of the new ego-identity yet more beautiful than before are no longer visible; when the new dreams no longer seem attainable, we know that the ego has regained control of the mental space.

We can either learn to remember who the new me is and enjoy living in the part of everything we are in, or we can learn to fly with a broken wing instead of playing the victim again, like when we were fighting. against the inevitable change believing to be going to our loss. It is an easy conscious choice to make.

Finally, we find joy, happiness and gratitude to live with our new identity by sharing and co-creating everywhere we go. This identity still remains an ego-identity, but the ego is no longer in control of the mental space. At least not as much. We know better how to recognize the ego as soon as it touches the steering wheel to control the path to follow. We know where to find our strength by connecting to our inner self. We bring our colors by doing good to all those who take the time to take the time with us. We flutter. We follow the path of nature.

During the transformation from caterpillar to butterfly, when new attributes and skills begin to kick in, the ego will fight hard not to lose control with false beliefs such as fluttering is not good.

not productive, or that these new colors will make us vulnerable to attacks making us also vulnerable to different prey, or even the fragility of our wings so it will be better to stay hidden as much as possible to avoid being injured.

These false beliefs will need to be transmuted for the butterfly to feel free and strong again. To flutter is to follow the flow of nature and to stop according to the inspirations to take the time to take the time, therefore, not to be under ego control. These stops are protective. Each butterfly has the colors that allow it to bring joy in its path and protect it from prey that will not see it. It is invisible to attackers. Although his wings may be fragile, they are strong and solid and will not prevent him from being a butterfly even if they break.

*A butterfly doesn't always have to fly
very high to be a butterfly.*

Throughout our lives, we change. Sometimes we transform by default, but we can also do it with will and mindfulness. How? By learning to free ourselves from thoughts that come from our ego.

That's what you've done here, learning to see what's coming from your ego and what's coming from your Inner Self.

Enjoy the beautiful continuity of your transformation!

Dr. Nathalie :)

These false beliefs will need to be transmuted for the butterfly to feel free and strong again. To flutter is to follow the flow of nature and to stop according to the inspirations to take the time to take the time, therefore, not to be under ego control. These stops are protective. Each butterfly has the colors that allow it to bring joy in its path and protect it from prey that will not see it. It is invisible to attackers. Although his wings may be fragile, they are strong and solid and will not prevent him from being a butterfly even if they break.

A butterfly doesn't always have to fly very high to be a butterfly.

Throughout our lives, we change. Sometimes we transform by default, but we can also do it with will and mindfulness. How? By learning to free ourselves from thoughts that come from our ego.

That's what you've done here, learning to see what's coming from your ego and what's coming from your Inner Self.

Enjoy the beautiful continuity of your transformation!

Dr. Nathalie :)

Thank you for taking the time for 31 days to lift the veils on your ego while seeing how the ego occupies your mental space. Raising the veils of your ego is becoming aware of a thought of the ego and choosing not to feed it anymore.
This is for your own well-being. You are doing this for no one but yourself and yes you will see some nice ripple effects as you keep your practice alive.
    Remember to **Breathe In**, let go of your ego-based thoughts and vision, see from your Soul, and **Love Out**!

    Dr. Nathalie

About the author

Dr. Nathalie began to fully embody her life mission when she decided to self-publish her first workbook in 2016. With no professional writing experience nor editor, she only knew that she had to start embodying her life mission in a different way. She always knew that writing was her passion, and over many decades since her first poems as a teenager, the many ideas for topics following her age and her overflowing imagination remained in her imagination or incomplete in her computer.

It is when she clearly understood her personal life mission that she jumped without a net, or rather with only a divine net as her only net in order to embody it by aligning herself with it, and this, despite a more or less clear action plan, and she started to fully assume her passion and her pleasure to be an author of personal development and spiritual awakening books.

Through gratitude and through her personal trials and personal life lessons which allowed her to become an expert in the art of remaining herself and of expressing her pleasure and her unconditional Love, she learned to develop an unconditional Gratitude Attitude.

Her unconditional Gratitude Attitude would have not been possible without a personal Inner connection through lots of meditation and Inner work over many decades.

Because she likes to learn and simplify things so that the ego does not interfere too much when learning different concepts or when the time comes to demystify the ego, and because one of her dreams is to allow everyone to have access to spiritual or metaphysical development and personal development information regardless of their budget and preferred method, she follows her inspirations by creating content to help people on their mindfulness journey by helping them from awareness to awakening, to then move from their awakening to reality allowing them to continue from an attitude of gratitude to Unity, to this interconnectivity and harmony with the Universe and the primary Source of the Universe.

Her teachings make it possible to understand that it is all a matter of understanding your ego so that you can lift up the ego veils, see with your Soul to choose your ego-identity aligned with your desires, and have an unconditional gratitude attitude.

To learn more about her tools and programs, visit nathalieturgeon.com .

breatheinloveoutcenter.com

www.ingramcontent.com/pod-product-compliance
Lightning Source LLC
Chambersburg PA
CBHW081122080526
44587CB00021B/3710